STUDY GUIDE

LIVING FREE FROM COMPARISON
AND THE NEED TO PLEASE

JOYCE MEYER

Faith
Words

NASHVILLE · NEW YORK

FaithWords
Hachette Book Group
1290 Avenue of the Americas, New York, NY 10104
faithwords.com
twitter.com/faithwords

First Edition: September 2021

FaithWords is a division of Hachette Book Group, Inc.
The FaithWords name and logo are trademarks of Hachette Book Group, Inc.

The publisher is not responsible for websites (or their content) that are not owned by the publisher.

The Hachette Speakers Bureau provides a wide range of authors for speaking events.
To find out more, go to www.hachettespeakersbureau.com or call (866) 376-6591.

ISBN: 978-1-5460-2639-6 (trade paperback)

Printed in the United States of America

LSC-C

Printing 1, 2021

CONTENTS

HOW TO USE THIS STUDY GUIDE

I am delighted that you have chosen to use this study guide that was designed as a companion to the book *Authentically, Uniquely You*. The lessons, principles, and stories contained in this book will equip and empower you to be the authentic and unique person God designed you to be. This study guide will help you get the maximum benefits from these teachings and learn to walk in the liberty to be and enjoy who you are without comparing yourself to or competing with other people.

As you read in the introduction of *Authentically, Uniquely You*, I spent many frustrating years trying to be like people I admired and trying to at least appear to be someone or something I was not. I had to learn that we are all unique and that there is no one else in the world exactly like us—and that makes us very special. We all need to discover and accept our own unique traits and to be free to embrace ourselves for who we really are.

You may know from personal experience that it is possible to try so hard to be like other people that you forget who you are. Perhaps you've allowed others to pressure you to become someone you are not, and you're frustrated with the struggle to meet those expectations. The good news is that Jesus came to set us free and offers us the liberty to be the amazing person He intends for us to be.

As you work through this study and reflect on your life, I strongly encourage you to read each chapter in *Authentically, Uniquely You* before you complete the exercises in the corresponding chapter in this study guide. In each chapter of this guide you will find the following four sections:

- **Get in Touch with Your Uniqueness** starts off each chapter, calling your attention to the opening quote and introducing you to the main points in the chapter. It sets the stage for you to dive deeper and understand how these words of wisdom can equip you to embrace and accept yourself.

- **Take Strength in God's Word** provides you with the powerful scriptures that are the source of all the principles in this book. Nothing is more important than exploring what God's Word says about each topic. You may want to make it a point to memorize any scripture that really speaks to you or says something you know you need to carry with you. Consider writing those scriptures on small cards or using sticky notes on your phone or computer to help you remember them.

- **Authenticity in Action** requires you to activate the principles you study by answering questions designed to help you reinforce or expand your understanding of the teaching in *Authentically, Uniquely You*. This section gives you an opportunity to reflect on your own personal journey.

- **Keep This in Mind** includes a brief summary of the main takeaway from each chapter, along with a scripture, to make it easy for you to remember this important principle and incorporate it into your life.

As you complete the activities in this study guide, I pray that you will receive one of the best gifts you can give yourself: accepting yourself and believing that God created you with His own hand, embracing your unique self, and living authentically. Be open and honest with yourself and with God, and you will find freedom from comparing yourself to others and from trying to please people in unhealthy ways. You will learn to set boundaries that keep you safe from letting others control or manipulate you, and you'll gain the courage to follow your own heart as God leads you forward. You're going to like who you are, and you'll enjoy being at peace with yourself.

I'm so thankful you have decided to take this journey that will lead to that amazing place where you can join David and say to God, "I praise you because I am fearfully and wonderfully made; your works are wonderful, I know that full well" (Psalm 139:14).

PART 1

Believing the Best about Yourself

CHAPTER 1

Learning to Love Who You Are

Get in Touch with Your Uniqueness

Love your neighbor as yourself.

Matthew 22:39

What is the pathway to authenticity? Explain why that is true.

_____

_____

What does it mean to love the unique you that God created you to be?

_____

_____

What was your immediate response to the question *Do you love yourself?*

_____

_____

If we don't love ourselves, why is it impossible to love God or anyone else?

_____

_____

How can you love yourself despite your flaws and imperfections?

_____

_____

When we don't love ourselves, we try to get the love we are missing from other people. What does that entail, and why does it never work?

_____

_____

Receiving God's love and loving yourself in a healthy, biblical way is the key to joy, peace, and confidence. Before you go any further, I encourage you to ask God to use this study guide and book to help you love yourself more than ever. Read John 13:23 and 21:7, 20. Do you have the confidence to refer to yourself in the same way John repeatedly referred to himself? How does knowing and living in the love of God make you powerful?

_____

_____

When we reject ourselves, what harmful cycle does it set up that must be broken in order to restore our authenticity?

_____

_____

Have you found that your own insecurities make it easy for others to manipulate and prey upon you? If yes, how so? To have the strength to healthy relationships, what must you have? And how can you protect yourself?

_____

_____

Instead of basing your beliefs about yourself on what others have told you or how they have behaved toward you, it's time for you to find out what God says about you in His Word and believe it.

Take Strength in God's Word

Read the following verses and write what God says about you in each one:
Zechariah 2:8

_____

_____

1 Corinthians 1:27; John 15:16

_____

_____

John 6:37

_____

_____

Jeremiah 31:3

_____

_____

1 Peter 2:9

_____

_____

1 Peter 4:10

_____

_____

2 Corinthians 5:21

_____

_____

Believing God's wonderful statements about you will change your life. Read John 14:6 and Hebrews 6:18. Why should you trust God and His Word?

_____

_____

Authenticity in Action

First Peter 3:11 states that we are to pursue peace with God, ourselves, and others. That means doing whatever it takes to maintain peace in our lives. Here are some ways you can activate and cultivate peace.

Receive God's forgiveness and be at peace with God. What is the best way to respond when you sin and are not at peace with Him?

_____

_____

Make the decision to like yourself. Write a prayer asking God to begin to show you the way He sees you and who He says you are.

_____

_____

_____

Don't compare yourself to others. Identify three areas of your life where you know you're comparing yourself to others and losing your peace and joy.

_____

_____

_____

Accept other people just the way they are. Describe one relationship in which you are trying or have tried to change a person into the way you want them to be.

_____

_____

_____

Let God have control of your life. Name an issue or situation in your life that you need to give to God and say, "My times are in your hands" (Psalm 31:15).

_____

_____

_____

To help identify areas of your life that are holding you back and that you need to focus on as you work through the rest of this study guide, take some time to ponder these questions, then rate yourself on a scale of 1 to 10, with 10 being the greatest amount.

- Do you believe that God loves you? 1 2 3 4 5 6 7 8 9 10
- Do you love and accept yourself? 1 2 3 4 5 6 7 8 9 10
- Are you a people-pleaser? 1 2 3 4 5 6 7 8 9 10

- Are you at peace with yourself?   1 2 3 4 5 6 7 8 9 10
- Do you fear rejection?   1 2 3 4 5 6 7 8 9 10
- Do you compare yourself with others?   1 2 3 4 5 6 7 8 9 10

Keep This in Mind

See what great love the Father has lavished on us, that we should be called children of God! And that is what we are!

1 John 3:1

When you live with the awareness that God loves you, and when you love yourself, there's no limit to what God can do through you or to the enjoyment you can find in your life.

CHAPTER 2

Your Self-Image Matters

Get in Touch with Your Uniqueness

The worst loneliness is not to be comfortable with yourself.

Mark Twain

Why is your self-image—how you see yourself—so important?

From the list of what the world teaches us to think, which points have had the most negative impact on your life?

By contrast, what does Jesus say about those specific points?

In the next two sections, you will focus on who you are in Christ and a healthy, godly view of yourself, but first focus on what happens when you think too little of yourself. Read Numbers 13:17–33. How did ten of the twelve spies view themselves, and how did that impact their lives and the lives of the Israelites?

Had you been one of the spies, do you see yourself siding with Joshua and Caleb or the other ten? What have your past experiences shown you about yourself?

_____

_____

Read 2 Samuel 9:1–13. How does Mephibosheth's response to King David's kindness reveal why he was living an impoverished life? Rather than see himself as disqualified from his position, how should he have viewed himself?

_____

_____

A poor self-image will keep you from being, doing, and having all that God has planned for you. Knowing who you are in Christ is extremely important.

Take Strength in God's Word

When we receive Jesus as our Savior, He comes to live in our spirit and our life is in Him. We _____ in Him by faith (John 15:5, 7), by believing what His Word says. Because God sees us "in Christ," every victory Jesus has won becomes our victory also. When He _____, we _____, and when He was _____, we too were _____ (Romans 6:4–5). He is _____ in the heavenly realms (Ephesians 1:20), and we are _____ in Him (Ephesians 2:6).

Read the following verses and write the important points made about who you are in Christ and consider how powerful your position is in Him:
2 Timothy 1:9

_____

_____

Ephesians 1:4

_____

_____

Ephesians 1:13

_____

_____

Romans 8:38–39

_____

_____

Ephesians 1:7

_____

_____

2 Corinthians 5:21

_____

_____

2 Corinthians 5:17

_____

_____

What do the following verses additionally tell you about who you are in Christ? Psalm 139:13–16; 1 Peter 1:18–19

_____

_____

Philippians 3:3

_____

_____

Philippians 4:13

_____

_____

Colossians 2:10

_____

_____

1 Corinthians 2:16

_____

_____

Ephesians 2:10

_____

_____

Romans 8:17

_____

_____

Romans 8:37

_____

_____

Though you may not feel like it today, you have to remember that you are in the process of growing into the person you already are in Christ. God sees you complete and finished. The Holy Spirit is working with and in you, transforming you into the image of Jesus (Romans 8:29), so be patient.

Authenticity in Action

Your view of yourself will determine your level of confidence, affect the way you evaluate the opportunities that come your way, and influence your relationships with God and others. From the list of bullet points in the "What Do You Think of Yourself" section, select six attitudes that you want to improve on in your life and write out bold declarations to help you renew your mind. Consider also writing these declarations on small cards or using sticky notes on your phone or computer to help you remember them.

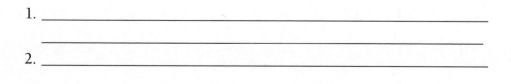

1. _____

_____

2. _____

_____

3. _____

_____

4. _____

_____

5. _____

_____

6. _____

_____

Keep This in Mind

Therefore, if anyone is in Christ, the new creation has come: The old has gone, the new is here!

2 Corinthians 5:17

What others think of you isn't nearly as important as what you think of yourself. Don't look at your weaknesses. Look at Jesus and His ability instead.

CHAPTER 3

Authenticity

Get in Touch with Your Uniqueness

These people honor me with their lips, but their hearts are far from me.

Matthew 15:8

What does it mean to be an authentic person?

_____

_____

Do you consider yourself to be an authentic person? Explain why. How would you like to improve in this area?

_____

_____

Read Matthew 23. Write down what you think are the three most important reasons Jesus gave for His scathing rebukes to the religious pretenders of His day.

_____

_____

Describe the contrast between the people in Isaiah 29:13 and the people whom Jesus describes in Matthew 22:37. Take some time to consider your own worship.

_____

_____

Write out Jesus' words in John 4:23–24, which define the only kind of worship that is acceptable to God. Meditate on what He is saying to you today.

_____

_____

How is our love and service to God brought into sharp focus in 1 Kings 18:21? What is it about the character of God that does not allow us to be people-pleasers?

_____

_____

Take Strength in God's Word

Scripture has much to say about being authentic in our service to God. What does Elijah say in 1 Kings 18:21 that makes it impossible for us to serve God?

_____

_____

Does 1 John 2:15 mean that if you are going to live fully committed to the Lord, you cannot enjoy the things in the world? Explain your answer.

_____

_____

In your life right now, are you making choices that align with Matthew 6:33? Spend some time praying about this. What is your heart telling you?

_____

_____

Write out the first half of Romans 12:9. To be *sincere* means to be *authentic*. Explain why you have pretended to love someone and were not sincere at times.

_____

_____

Read Matthew 6:1–6. On a scale of 1 to 10, with 1 being "very poor" and 10 being "exceptional," how do you rate yourself at not telling anyone when you have done good things for people? Why do we find this so difficult to do?

_____

_____

What do 1 Peter 1:22 (AMPC) and 1 John 3:18 (AMPC) specifically tell us really matters about our love and why we are doing what we are doing?

_____

_____

Authenticity in Action

I want you to apply this lesson on authenticity to your friendships. What values of authenticity do you most desire in your friends?

_____

_____

If you want authentic friendships, what do Matthew 7:1–2, 5:7, and 7:12 tell you that you first must be?

_____

_____

According to James 3:10, what warning do you need to heed about what you say about other people?

_____

_____

Proverbs 17:17 states an incredibly important characteristic of a true friend. Describe a time when a friend supported you through a time of adversity. What did that mean to you?

_____

_____

When you hear something bad about a friend, what should you first do (see 2 Corinthians 13:1)? If it is true, what should you not do?

_____

_____

Do you have friends and family members who tell other people's secrets and spread gossip? Why must you be cautious what you say and do around them?

_____

_____

_____

Read Ruth 1. Describe how Ruth exemplifies being an authentic friend.

_____

_____

In what amazing way was Ruth rewarded for her faithfulness to Naomi?

_____

_____

Read 2 Kings 2:1–14. How was Elisha a true friend to the prophet Elijah, and what blessing came to him as a result?

_____

_____

_____

Describe one of your relationships in which a friend needs you to stand with them and support them through a rough time. Make a commitment to remain faithful.

_____

_____

Write out Hebrews 13:5, then apply that to one situation in your life where you feel as though you're on your own and you need help.

_____

_____

To be an authentic person and a powerful witness for God, declare out loud that you will:

- Have _____ (Psalm 24:3–5; Matthew 5:8).
- Be _____ (Proverbs 21:21; 1 Timothy 1:5).
- Tell _____ (Ephesians 4:25; Colossians 3:9).
- Live _____ (Proverbs 6:16–20; 2 Corinthians 8:21).

Keep This in Mind

Jesus replied: "'Love the Lord your God with all your heart and with all your soul and with all your mind.'"

Matthew 22:37

To be authentic means to be genuine and real in every area of your life, not to be a pretender. Authentic people don't behave one way with some people and another way with other people simply to fit in, impress, or be accepted.

CHAPTER 4

Uniquely You

Get in Touch with Your Uniqueness

You're born an original, don't die a copy!

John Mason

Why is it so hard to believe that you were "born an original" and not a copy?

_____

_____

_____

How does Psalm 139 confirm that you were "born an original"?

_____

_____

_____

Based upon Isaiah 46:10 and Philippians 1:6, if you agree and cooperate with God, what amazing promise are you given? How does this encourage you?

_____

_____

_____

Being your unique self requires that you "follow the guidance of the Holy Spirit" rather than other people. What do you think that means?

_____

_____

Take Strength in God's Word

Why can you be confident that you can hear from God and not be fearful that you will somehow miss His guidance?

_____

_____

How does James 1:5 affirm that God desires to guide you into all He has for you?

_____

_____

What does James mean when he says that God gives us wisdom "generously" and "without finding fault"? How does that encourage you to ask in faith and not be double-minded?

_____

_____

Psalm 31:3 says that God will lead and guide you for the sake of His name. What is His name connected to, and what powerful assurance comes with that?

_____

_____

Isaiah 30:21 teaches that God's voice of guidance is real and specific. How do you hear His voice?

_____

_____

Read 1 Kings 19:12 in several translations. In a time of turmoil in his life, what did Elijah have to do to hear God's voice, and what did he hear?

_____

_____

God guides you to be your unique self by the desires He puts in your heart. Why is it so important that you realize how God has gifted you and to guard _your_ life?

_____

_____

Why must you be courageous enough to be true to yourself?

_____

_____

Describe why it is a mistake to try to get other people to do what God has led you to do or to do it that way. Why is it a mistake if you try to do it their way?

_____

_____

What can happen if you pressure a person into conforming to your life path?

_____

_____

Authenticity in Action

Ralph Waldo Emerson said, "To be yourself in a world that is constantly trying to make you someone else is the greatest accomplishment." Trying to make others be what we want them to be or succumbing to their pressure to make us be what they want us to be is a major reason relationships fail.

Describe a past situation in your life where you allowed pressure for the approval of another person to try to change yourself into someone you are not. What outcome did you experience?

_____

_____

What are you learning about yourself that will keep you from allowing it to recur?

_____

_____

If you don't like yourself, why are you destined for a life of misery?

_____

_____

Why is *believing* that God loves you so incredibly important? Take some time and really examine how you feel and what you believe about yourself.

_____

_____

Amos 3:3 states that the only way to walk with God is to agree with Him about *everything* He says. Write out your agreement with what He says in Genesis 1:31.

_____

_____

Write out your agreement with what God says in Psalm 139:16.

_____

_____

God told Jeremiah that before He formed him in the womb that He knew and approved of him as His "chosen instrument" (Jeremiah 1:5 AMPC). Write out how you can apply this same truth when you face your imperfections and mistakes.

_____

_____

God accepts us as we are and then goes about the work of changing us to be the best version of ourselves that we can be. Write down Hebrews 12:6 and begin to commit it to memory as the gentle and timely way God corrects and changes us.

_____

_____

Describe how God corrects us. What is He welcoming us into, and why are His method and timing perfect?

_____

_____

Write down some of the ways God has brought correction to you.

_____

_____

What is the only way that you will experience real change in your life?

_____

_____

Before you close this chapter, invite God to work in you, to bring correction in His time and His way. Receive it joyfully as His loving gift to you.

Keep This in Mind

The word of the Lord came to me, saying, "Before I formed you in the womb I knew you, before you were born I set you apart."

Jeremiah 1:4–5

In order to be your unique self, accept the fact that God loves you just the way you are and simply ask Him to make you what He wants you to be. Know that this is *your* life, and who you are is given as a gift from God. Be true to yourself.

CHAPTER 5

You Are Exceptional

Get in Touch with Your Uniqueness

For with God nothing will be impossible.

Luke 1:37 NKJV

Have you ever thought of yourself as exceptional, as full of possibilities? How does this statement by Jesus cause you to see yourself?

_____

_____

Read Genesis 12:1–3. What propelled Abraham from being an ordinary man to becoming "the father of many nations"?

_____

_____

What powerful encouragement can you take away from what God did in and through Abraham's life?

_____

_____

I encourage you to dare to dream big, because God is "able to do immeasurably more than all we ask or imagine" (Ephesians 3:20). It starts by asking God to do great things. Write a declaration that this is what you're believing for.

_____

_____

What assurance do you have that your weaknesses cannot stop God?

_____

_____

Paul instructed the Romans to offer their "bodies [presenting all your members and faculties] as a living sacrifice" to God (Romans 12:1 AMPC). Perhaps you have given everything you are to God to use as He pleases. Have you given Him everything you are not? Consider this prayerfully, and write your prayer below.

_____

_____

Name a weakness in your life that you know has been holding you back and that you are giving to God to use for His glory.

_____

_____

Read Matthew 14:13–21. What do you need to remember from this story?

_____

_____

Describe the level of power you have according to God's promise in James 4:7.

_____

_____

Take Strength in God's Word

God's Word is filled with ordinary people who did extraordinary feats. Name your favorite biblical character and why they are special to you.

_____

_____

God's anointing—His presence, ability, and power on us—qualifies and enables us to do certain things. How does His anointing go beyond your natural talents?

_____

_____

Read Isaiah 10:27 (NKJV). What does this verse tell you the anointing does?

_____

_____

Jesus was called the "Anointed One" (Mark 8:29; Acts 26:23; Ephesians 4:15 AMPC). Describe both the Old and New Testament concept of the *anointing*.

_____

_____

What do 1 John 2:20 and 27 tell us about the role of the anointing in our lives? Does this mean that you no longer need others to teach you the Word?

_____

_____

Read Luke 4:18–19. The fact that Jesus was anointed for ministry makes it clear that we all need God's anointing. From the list of gifts given in Romans 12:4–8, do you sense that God has anointed you in one area of service? Are you using your gift now to serve others? How can you improve in this area?

_____

_____

Authenticity in Action

Although we all want to do great things for the Lord, where did Jesus say it all begins (see Luke 16:10)?

_____

_____

You read how God led me through a long progression of small steps over forty-five years into the worldwide ministry we have today. Write out the first half of Zechariah 4:10 (NLT). No matter how far along you are in your ministry, how does this verse encourage you for every step of your journey?

_____

_____

We tend to think about all the great miracles Jesus performed, but He also did a lot of small things. What did He do in the following verses:

John 13:4–5

_____

_____

John 21:9

_____

_____

John 2:1–11

_____

_____

Luke 19:1–5

_____

_____

John 11:35

_____

_____

We are often too busy being religious to stop and help those in need, but Jesus wasn't. How can you improve in this area?

_____

_____

In Luke 21:1–4, what is Jesus telling us that makes His heart glad in our giving? Do you believe that is equally true when it comes to your giving and service?

_____

_____

Read Matthew 21:1–10. Even Jesus' triumphal entry into Jerusalem was an act of humility. What lesson is He teaching us for when we triumph and are being successful in what He has called us to do?

_____

_____

No matter how little you have or think you can do, offer it to God, be faithful over it, and He will do great things (Matthew 25:23). You are exceptional, and you will do extraordinary things because all things are possible with God.

Keep This in Mind

Now to him who is able to do immeasurably more than all we ask or imagine, according to his power that is at work within us.

Ephesians 3:20

To be exceptional means to be outstanding and beyond ordinary, and every child of God—including you—fits that description. You cannot comprehend how great your life can be with God, because the possibilities are limitless.

CHAPTER 6

If at First You Don't Succeed, You're Normal!

Get in Touch with Your Uniqueness

Only those who dare to fail greatly can ever achieve greatly.

Robert F. Kennedy

On a scale of 1 to 10, with 1 being "very afraid" and 10 being "bring it on," how do you rate yourself when it comes to stepping out of your comfort zone in order to achieve success at something you've never done before? Explain.

What is the key to eventually succeeding after we've tried and failed?

Read through the stories of Thomas Edison, Abraham Lincoln, Walt Disney, and Milton Hershey. What inspiration can you take from their lives?
Thomas Edison

Abraham Lincoln

Walt Disney

_____

_____

Milton Hershey

_____

_____

Describe a situation in your life when God took your mistake and turned it into a life lesson or even made a miracle out of it.

_____

_____

What keeps a failure from making you into a failure?

_____

_____

Explain the meaning of John Maxwell's statement that you can "fail forward."

_____

_____

Take Strength in God's Word

The Bible is filled with stories of people who failed miserably and ended up being used by God greatly. What does Proverbs 24:16 tell you is the way to success?

_____

_____

Read 1 Kings 17–18 and document the extraordinary victories and miracles that the prophet Elijah performed. Imagine experiencing all that he did there.

_____

_____

Keep reading Elijah's story in 1 Kings 19:1–18. What followed his incredible successes? Did that make him a failure? What was God's response to all this?

_____

_____

What did King David's epic failure involve? Take the time to read 2 Samuel 11:2–12:13.

_____

_____

What do you take away from Acts 13:22 that brought David through this tragic episode in his life, an experience that would have ruined most people?

_____

_____

What encouragement do you get from reading the account of John Mark's failure in Acts 13:13 and 15:37–40 and in Colossians 4:10–11?

_____

_____

Who failed in the following verses, and how did they fail?
Luke 22:61

_____

_____

Exodus 11:8; 32:19

_____

_____

Acts 8:3; Galatians 1:13

_____

_____

Ruth 1:16–22

_____

_____

Thank God that the way we begin in life is not the way we have to end.

Authenticity in Action

What is the primary reason most people don't try new things?

_____

What fundamental change do we need to make in our perspective on failure?

_____

_____

To become the best version you can be of yourself, what is it that you want to do with or in your life that you have not yet done?

_____

_____

Do you love your work, or would you really like to try something else? Why?

_____

_____

Do you love your life, or do you waste your time wishing you had someone else's existence? Give an honest evaluation of what you are feeling.

_____

_____

Are you longing to try a new hairstyle or look but concerned the new one might not be as good as the old one? What's keeping you back?

_____

_____

Gaining a new perspective requires a new way of thinking about yourself and your life. Respond to how applying the following suggestions can help you start living the life you desire.

1. Let go of perfection.

_____

_____

2. Get to know yourself.

_____

_____

3. Allow yourself to be vulnerable.

_____

_____

4. Stop hiding.

_____

_____

5. Be your own best friend.

_____

_____

6. Find your own group.

_____

_____

7. Ask for help.

_____

_____

8. Doubt your doubts.

_____

_____

Keep This in Mind

For though the righteous fall seven times, they rise again.

Proverbs 24:16

If you never give up, you will eventually find your sweet spot. As you search for it, remember that failing at something doesn't make you a failure.

CHAPTER 7

What's Right with You?

Get in Touch with Your Uniqueness

God made him who had no sin to be sin for us, so that in him we might become the righteousness of God.

2 Corinthians 5:21

What was your immediate response to Paul's statement that you have "become the righteousness of God"? Do you know what it means? Do you believe it?

_____

_____

Does the message *What is wrong with me?* play in your head? In what ways have you been made to feel as though something is wrong with you?

_____

_____

What is the fundamental truth that people who have been mistreated, rejected, or abused need to know about themselves?

_____

_____

What happens when we are stuck in the mindset that something is wrong with us?

_____

_____

Take Strength in God's Word

One of the first gifts God gives us through salvation is righteousness. He wants us to know He views us as in right standing with Him because of our faith in Jesus, which gives us joy and also produces peace (Romans 5:1).

What qualifies you for God's righteousness according to Romans 3:23–24?

_____

_____

_____

Write out a clear definition of what it means to be "justified."

_____

_____

_____

According to Romans 3:24, we are justified by _____, that justification is based on the _____, accomplished through _____ (Romans 5:9), and brought to us through _____ (Romans 4:25).

Why does it take time to make righteousness a reality in our daily walk?

_____

_____

Write a prayer for an understanding of the right kind of righteousness based on the apostle Paul's prayer in Philippians 3:9.

_____

_____

Have you made religious rules you must keep or you will feel guilty? Has your church added to the list of rules to follow? Name those rules.

_____

_____

_____

Studying God's Word and spending time in prayer are both very important and profitable, but what happens when you make a law out of them? What truths about both will help you keep these from becoming a burden rather than a joy?

_____

_____

What does Ephesians 2:10 tell us we were created to do? What should your motive be in doing them? Do you earn points in the process?

_____

_____

Read Isaiah 61:3, Luke 4:18, Romans 8:15, and Hebrews 2:14–15. What is "the great exchange" we make with God?

_____

_____

Write down Romans 8:17 and begin to commit it to memory.

_____

_____

What does it mean that you have an inheritance in Christ? Meditate on this profound truth.

_____

_____

Everything God has is made available to us, not because we have anything to offer in exchange but because God is good.

Authenticity in Action

Ephesians 6:10–18 tells us how we are to put on righteousness and defeat our enemy, the devil. Give a simple explanation for what it means to put on each piece of the armor that God has supplied us.

Belt of truth

_____

_____

Breastplate of righteousness

_____

_____

Shoes of peace

_____

Shield of faith

_____

_____

Helmet of salvation

_____

_____

Sword of the Spirit, the Word of God

_____

_____

All kinds of prayer in the Spirit

_____

_____

What does it mean to "wear righteousness"? Does it mean to overlook sin?

_____

_____

What does wearing righteousness empower and set you free to be?

_____

_____

How does the truth of 2 Corinthians 5:17 (AMPC) free us from feeling that we must struggle and struggle to produce our own right behavior?

_____

_____

What makes you full of wonderful possibilities, pregnant with possibilities?

_____

_____

If you have the Father's DNA, spiritually, in you, and you have His calling to represent Him to others (2 Corinthians 5:20), what should they see when they see you? How is this possible?

_____

_____

I want to close by urging you to stop trying to be something you already are. Write a prayer asking God to simply show you how to walk by the Spirit instead of by the flesh and to allow good fruit to be produced in abundance.

_____

_____

Keep This in Mind

Therefore, since we have been justified through faith, we have peace with God through our Lord Jesus Christ.

Romans 5:1

Through faith in Christ, not keeping all the rules of religion, you are righteous in God's sight. No matter how you may fail or what your weaknesses may be, you can freely walk in God's love, approval, and acceptance.

CHAPTER 8

Make Peace with Yourself

Get in Touch with Your Uniqueness

If it is possible, as far as it depends on you, live at peace with everyone.

Romans 12:18

Living at peace "with everyone" includes yourself. Are you living at peace with yourself, or are you angry with yourself much of the time? Take some time to think about this. Explain what you are feeling.

_____

_____

What difference does it make whether you are at peace with yourself or not?

_____

_____

What powerful reason do we have to be at peace with ourselves?

_____

_____

From the thirteen bullet points of advice on how to think healthy, godly thoughts, write down the four points that you know you need to most focus on.

_____

_____

What is the problem with having yourself on your mind too much? Where should your thoughts be centered?

_____

_____

If you are angry with yourself, what is causing it? Consider this prayerfully.

_____

_____

If you are one of the many people who don't like themselves because they don't like the way they look, how can you make peace with whatever you don't like?

_____

_____

Why shouldn't you make excuses for doing things you know you shouldn't do? What difference does it make when you own your problems?

_____

_____

Some people are slower than we are to get things done, or they take longer to make decisions, or they do something differently than how we do it, and we find it irritating. Rather than see them as flawed, how should we see them?

_____

_____

Take Strength in God's Word

From 1 Peter 3:11, what does it mean to "seek" or "search for" peace?

_____

_____

Have you ever thought about how many of your problems with people are rooted in problems you have with yourself? Write down a few issues where you see this playing out in your relationships.

_____

_____

Read 1 Samuel 16:7. When God looks at you, what is more important to Him than your behavior? What difference can this truth make in your life today?

_____

_____

What does Philippians 3:13 tell you that you must do with your past mistakes?

_____

_____

If you have repented of any sin, no matter what it was, God has forgiven you and forgotten what you did. What do the following verses tell you God has done?

Psalm 103:12

_____

_____

Hebrews 8:12

_____

_____

Romans 3:24

_____

_____

God has forgiven and forgotten your sins, but do you remember them and let them trouble and anger you? Write a declaration of commitment to do as He has done.

_____

_____

According to John 6:28–29, what is one work that you must do? Do you add *Yes, and what else?* to what Jesus stated?

_____

_____

Read John 11:38–44. What principle is involved in experiencing God's power?

_____

_____

Authenticity in Action

The fulfillment of God's promises, whether it is that your sins have been forgiven and completely washed away, or that He loves you unconditionally, or that God is taking care of your problems, comes by faith and patience and through continuing to believe while you wait.

Write down the wonderful promise in Romans 15:13 that comes with waiting.

_____

_____

What does Jesus promise you in Mark 11:24? What test comes along with it?

_____

_____

If you find yourself in God's waiting room, what do you need to tell yourself?

_____

_____

Do you often find yourself trying to get what God has already stated He has given? Rather than try to get peace, what do you need to do? And if a lack of peace continues, what does John 14:27 tell you to do?

_____

_____

Do you keep praying over and over for the same sin to be forgiven? What must you do to put an end to the cycle of guilt?

_____

_____

Write down John 16:24, then take some time right now to sit quietly in God's presence and receive by faith His love, peace, joy, healing, and any other of His promises you need. Write a prayer of thanksgiving.

Keep This in Mind

Stop allowing yourselves to be agitated and disturbed; and do not permit yourselves to be fearful and intimidated and cowardly and unsettled.

John 14:27 AMPC

Being at peace with yourself is dependent upon thinking healthy, godly thoughts about who you are in Christ. You have peace as a gift from God, but you must choose to walk in it every day. Your part is simply to keep believing.

PART 2

Finding the Freedom to Be Yourself

CHAPTER 9

Don't Let Your Soul Take Control

Get in Touch with Your Uniqueness

For the word of God is alive and active. Sharper than any double-edged sword, it penetrates even to dividing soul and spirit, joints and marrow; it judges the thoughts and attitudes of the heart.

Hebrews 4:12

What is the difference between the soul and the spirit?

_____

_____

To live authentically, why must you learn to follow the Holy Spirit of God, who leads you through your spirit?

_____

_____

Describe how God uses a sense of peace to guide you into His will.

_____

_____

How do you make the transition from a life controlled by your soul to a life under the control of the Holy Spirit?

_____

_____

In your journey with God, have you learned that you can control your soul? What areas of your life do you struggle with the most?

_____

_____

Take Strength in God's Word

Read Galatians 5:16–26 and John 14:15. What is the key to walking in the Spirit?

_____

_____

In Psalm 23:2 and Isaiah 61:3 and 7, what three promises does God give you about wounds and pains and brokenness you may have in your soul?

_____

_____

Why must you have a soul that is whole in order to live out of your authentic self?

_____

_____

According to John 15:5, what is your source of strength to doing God's will?

_____

_____

What does Hebrews 4:12 tell you the Word of God will do for you?

_____

_____

Read 1 Timothy 6:12 and Romans 12:2. What two things must be done in order to be free from being controlled by the soul?

_____

_____

Prayerfully consider 2 Corinthians 10:4–5. How can you apply this powerful truth to your everyday experiences?

_____

What must you be prepared to do in this fight of faith to think the right thoughts and do the right thing (Hebrews 12:3; Galatians 6:9)?

_____

_____

Describe a typical situation where you know you should say no to doing something, but your mind and emotions push you hard to give in. What happens every time you stand firm and do what you should?

_____

_____

Authenticity in Action

We all struggle with people-pleasing. Take some time to identify and write down the root of your problem.

_____

_____

What truth will bring you freedom from being a people-pleaser?

_____

_____

Overcoming a problem such as people-pleasing can never come from using your willpower alone. What vital lesson is found in the quote from Watchman Nee?

_____

_____

Describe the insight given in Romans 6:12–13 on what happens when you yield to God and the role of grace in your everyday walk.

_____

_____

Write down the second half of Galatians 3:3 and begin to commit it to memory.

_____

_____

What two amazing things does the grace of God do for you?

_____

_____

Describe the steps you need to take to change your life from a wrong behavior.

_____

_____

How can you accept and enjoy yourself even while you are still imperfect?

_____

_____

How can you deal with the temptation to please people instead of God from now on?

_____

_____

Keep This in Mind

So I say, walk by the Spirit, and you will not gratify the desires of the flesh.
Galatians 5:16

The only way to live authentically is to learn to follow the Holy Spirit of God, who leads you through your spirit. As you grow in spiritual maturity, submitting to the will of God, your soul *gradually* comes under the control of the Holy Spirit.

CHAPTER 10

The Need for Approval

Get in Touch with Your Uniqueness

A man cannot be comfortable without his own approval.

Mark Twain

It's one thing to acknowledge that you should never sacrifice your authenticity to gain the approval of other people, but how do you actually do that?

_____

_____

Read Jeremiah 1:5 (AMPC). What does that tell you about God's approval of you?

_____

_____

Describe what it means to be a member of God's family.

_____

_____

In order to approve of yourself, what type of decisions must you be making?

_____

_____

Describe some of the ways you give up your own happiness in an effort to keep others happy and pleased with you. What is the outcome when you do?

_____

_____

When someone makes a request of you that you know you should say no to, what must you do to keep from saying yes simply to please that person?

_____

_____

What is the problem with always saying yes to those who ask something of you?

_____

_____

Take Strength in God's Word

It is impossible to please all people all of the time. What does Colossians 3:15 state should guide our yes and our no in all our decisions?

_____

_____

What does Romans 15:1–2 state about pleasing other people? How far does that principle go?

_____

_____

Define what it means to have an approval addiction.

_____

_____

Do you find yourself looking for an approval "fix" when you are feeling insecure?

_____

_____

What does Ephesians 3:17 state is the cure for approval addiction?

_____

_____

Describe the foundation for your security and confidence in the following verses:

_____

_____

Romans 5:1

_____

_____

Romans 5:21

_____

_____

2 Corinthians 5:17

_____

_____

Authenticity in Action

Our society today suffers from an epidemic of insecurity, and many people often seek others' approval to alleviate the pain of low self-esteem. On a scale of 1 to 10, with 1 being "very needy" and 10 being "fully confident," how do you rate yourself? Explain what you are feeling.

_____

_____

Several examples are given in this chapter of a person whose need for another person's approval caused them to conform rather than face rejection or disapproval. Describe an area of your life in which you struggle.

_____

_____

Based on what you are learning, what truth about that situation will help you remain true to following your own desires the next time you face this?

_____

_____

If you can't be happy unless someone encourages or compliments you about something, what is the problem?

_____

_____

If you battle the pain of low self-esteem, what happens when you seek others' attention and approval to try to feel better?

_____

_____

What is the only lasting foundation that gives you the security and confidence that is guaranteed to satisfy your inner needs?

_____

_____

Write a prayer of thanksgiving for the privilege as God's child of trusting His unconditional love and His process of making you into all He wants you to be.

_____

_____

Keep This in Mind

If I were still trying to please people, I would not be a servant of Christ.
Galatians 1:10

Never sacrifice your authenticity to gain the approval of other people. Believe that God approves of you, and approve of yourself. Always separate your *who* from your *do*.

CHAPTER 11

Freedom from Comparison

Get in Touch with Your Uniqueness

Comparison is the death of joy.

Mark Twain

Why is it a mistake to compare yourself to someone else and try to do what they do or try to be someone you were never meant to be?

_____

_____

What was your immediate response to the statement that the company CEO and janitor are both equally valuable to God? Do you see people the same way?

_____

_____

How does the devil tempt you to compare yourself to others?

_____

_____

Why is it true that "comparison is the death of joy"?

Take Strength in God's Word

Read John 3:22–30. What made John's disciples feel insecure?

_____

What truth did John understand that kept him free from their insecurity (v. 27)?

_____

_____

Where did John find his joy even when his popularity waned (vv. 28–30)?

_____

_____

When is it not a problem to compare ourselves with other people?

_____

_____

As was true for John the Baptist, what does Hebrews 12:2 tell you brings freedom from insecurity?

_____

_____

Read 1 Corinthians 12:4–11 in *The Message* translation. What does it tell about the immensity and creativity of God in your uniqueness?

_____

_____

How is that same truth reflected in all of nature? Read Genesis 1:20–25.

_____

_____

Given God's creativity, describe why it is an insult to Him when we try to be like someone else.

_____

Authenticity in Action

God has given people different temperaments, with a variety of sub-traits that make us uniquely different. We should celebrate our differences rather than wish we were like someone else or try to make someone else be like us. This is the only way we can ever truly be free to be ourselves as well as get along with other people and enjoy healthy relationships with them.

From the description of the four different temperament types, which temperament are you? Explain why you see yourself this way.

_____

Name and describe someone you know who is sanguine.

_____

Name and describe someone you know who is choleric.

_____

Name and describe someone you know who is melancholy.

_____

Name and describe someone you know who is phlegmatic.

_____

What are you learning about accepting others and helping them feel valuable?

_____

Do you see yourself in the short story of the crow? How so?

_____

What vital lesson can you take away from that story?

_____

Write a prayer asking God to help you recognize, appreciate, and value all the positive aspects of who you are and everything that is good about other people.

_____

Keep This in Mind

Fixing our eyes on Jesus, the pioneer and perfecter of faith.

Hebrews 12:2

Enjoy being the person you are without comparing yourself to anyone else, trying to do what they do, or trying to be someone you were never meant to be. You are valuable to God for *who you are*, not for *what you do.*

CHAPTER 12

Are You Stuck in the Control Trap?

Get in Touch with Your Uniqueness

True love is built on free will and free choice, not control and manipulation.

Ken Poirot

Describe what you have experienced when being under the influence of a controller. How did it impact your thinking and the expression of your true feelings?

_____

_____

Why is it important that you understand how control operates?

_____

_____

If you have allowed someone to control you, explain why you stayed under their control.

_____

_____

Why is breaking free from control so hard to do?

_____

_____

Describe a person who controls others.

_____

_____

What is the primary way that people try to control others? Explain.

_____

_____

If you can relate to my story and are hungry for healing and freedom in your life, you may learn some helpful lessons from my books *Healing the Soul of a Woman* and *Beauty for Ashes*.

Take Strength in God's Word

Read 1 Samuel 25:1–38. From the list of characteristics of a controlling person in Les Parrott III's book *The Control Freak*, write down the ones that are evident in the brief story of the man named Nabal and expand upon them.

_____

_____

Why do you think Abigail had stayed with him?

_____

_____

What was it that finally caused her to take a stand that would risk his fury?

_____

_____

Authenticity in Action

From the list of ten characteristics of a controlling person, describe two characteristics in controllers that have troubled you the most.

_____

_____

In what ways have you been ordered around by a controller? How did you respond?

_____

_____

In what ways have you faced the volatility of a controller's anger? How did you respond?

_____

_____

In what ways have you been manipulated by a controller to make you feel guilty or as though you owe them something? How did you respond?

_____

_____

Why is it true that the longer you allow someone to control you, the more difficult it is to break free from their grasp?

_____

_____

Why is it impossible to live an authentic life if you are under someone's control?

_____

_____

Having studied this chapter, are you presently in a relationship with someone who is exercising some level of control over you? If so, write a bold declaration that you will not continue to live this way and that you will find a way to break free and live under the influence and guidance of the Holy Spirit.

_____

_____

Keep This in Mind

For God has not given us a spirit of fear, but of power and of love and of a sound mind.

2 Timothy 1:7 NKJV

If you are being controlled, you have a responsibility to stop it. As long as you allow it to go on, you enable abusive behavior.

CHAPTER 13

Breaking Free from the Power of Control

Get in Touch with Your Uniqueness

The boundary lines have fallen for me in pleasant places.

Psalm 16:6

Why is it important for you to learn the importance of boundary lines in your relationships?

_____

_____

If you have been damaged from the abusive treatment of a controller, what must happen in order for freedom and healing to come?

_____

_____

When you confront a controller, what must you be willing to face?

_____

_____

Have you ever confronted a controller? If so, what was their response?

_____

_____

Take Strength in God's Word

Confronting a controller can be very difficult, but what does Luke 18:27 tell you about working through the problem? Explain.

_____

_____

Read 1 Corinthians 7:15–16. What general principle does the apostle Paul give regarding how we deal with a person who is mistreating us?

_____

_____

Read 1 Corinthians 13:4–7. In what ways does a controller fail to love and respect you?

_____

_____

If you begin to set and keep boundaries in the relationship, why might the controller become angry? See John 3:20.

_____

_____

If you confront a controller who is willing to work on the problem, what does Galatians 5:1 remind you to do during this difficult process that takes some time?

_____

_____

Authenticity in Action

While the emphasis in this chapter has been on those who try to control you, have you been the controller in some relationships? In what ways?

_____

_____

_____

When you have tried to control others, why did you feel the need to do it?

_____

_____

_____

Has anyone ever confronted you when you tried to control them and get your way? How did you respond?

_____

_____

_____

To change a controlling behavior, what is required of you for God to work?

_____

_____

_____

Search your heart and ask God to reveal to you how much time you waste being upset about petty situations and to show you how much better it would be to simply let them go. Write down your thoughts about this.

_____

_____

_____

Is all control wrong if it means doing something we don't want to do or something with which we don't agree? Explain your answer within the context of a wife's relationship to her husband.

_____

_____

_____

How do you remain in balance within a relationship when you disagree with each other's positions?

_____

_____

_____

Before you confront a situation, what do you need to do ever so prayerfully?

_____

_____

_____

Keep This in Mind

Have nothing to do with the fruitless deeds of darkness, but rather expose them.

Ephesians 5:11

Control issues that are hidden in the dark must be exposed to the light in order for freedom and healing to come. You have the right and responsibility to set boundaries in your relationships and not let people take advantage of you.

CHAPTER 14

You Can't Please Everyone, Part 1

Get in Touch with Your Uniqueness

Don't worry about who doesn't like you, who has more, or who's doing what.

Erma Bombeck

What is the difference between living to be a blessing to people and living to please people?

_____

_____

What do you think of yourself? Do you like yourself and appreciate your uniqueness? Would you say you have a healthy self-image? Explain.

_____

_____

Do you find yourself often looking to others to tell you that you are acceptable and that you have worth and value? What is the problem that this creates?

_____

_____

If you always have to be first or to be better than others, what are you missing inside, and how does it keep you from being authentic?

_____

_____

Take Strength in God's Word

What do the following verses tell you about people-pleasing?
Philippians 2:7

_____

_____

John 7:4–6

_____

_____

Mark 3:21

_____

_____

Galatians 1:10

_____

_____

1 Thessalonians 2:4

_____

_____

2 Timothy 4:3

_____

_____

John 12:42–43

_____

_____

Why will you not be able to be authentic as long as you must please other people?

_____

_____

Authenticity in Action

Read Colossians 3:23–24, then take some time to be still and ask yourself whether you are living to please yourself, other people, or God. Write an honest review.

_____

_____

When you know that God wants you to be more committed in an area of your life to Him but your friends wouldn't approve, how have you responded? Describe.

_____

_____

What does John 15:18 tell us to expect when we live fully committed to Jesus?

_____

_____

Are you willing to lose friends if necessary in order to go deeper with God? Have you lost friends in the past? Describe your experience.

_____

_____

Rather than let rejection from people hinder you from following God's leading in your life, what did Jesus state in Luke 10:1–17 that you should do?

_____

_____

The list of other people's expectations upon your life is seemingly endless. How hard is it for you to say no to some requests? Is it a problem? Why?

_____

_____

What about your expectations of other people? Do you feel they are obligated to say yes to your requests? Are you disappointed by a no? Explain what you feel.

_____

_____

What do Acts 7:25 and Genesis 37:3–4 teach about your expectations of others? Why is important that you communicate your expectations to others?

_____

_____

To be happy, what is the best thing you can do with your expectations of others?

_____

_____

Do you routinely set aside your own legitimate needs in order to please others? Describe some of the ways you do it.

_____

_____

When you deny your own needs this way, what does it lead to? Explain.

_____

_____

What change in your thinking will help you live a balanced life in this area?

_____

_____

Write out Acts 5:29 and begin to commit it to memory. What makes this such an important principle for you to heed?

_____

_____

When you say no to someone's request and they react negatively, what truth about the situation will keep you from allowing them to control you?

_____

_____

What behavior makes a people-pleaser into a dishonest person?

_____

_____

How does Ephesians 4:15 express that people-pleasing behavior is dishonorable?

_____

_____

If you have been a people-pleaser and are ready to change, what can you expect from those who demand you to do their bidding? Are you prepared for what it might cost you in your relationships?

_____

_____

If someone doesn't want to be your friend because you no longer allow them to control you, what is the truth about them?

_____

_____

Keep This in Mind

We are not trying to please people but God, who tests our hearts.

1 Thessalonians 2:4

Why struggle to gain acceptance and approval from others since God already accepts you, approves of you, and loves you with a perfect love? Don't allow people-pleasing to steal your destiny or stunt your spiritual growth.

CHAPTER 15

You Can't Please Everyone, Part 2

Get in Touch with Your Uniqueness

The price of greatness is responsibility.

Winston Churchill

People-pleasing exacts a great cost to your uniqueness and authenticity. Let's take a closer look at the requirements of a people-pleaser, and then you can decide if it is worth it to you.

To respect yourself, what qualities must you have in yourself?

_____

_____

What happens if you say yes to someone's request when your heart says no?

_____

_____

What do feelings of guilt and shame lead to when someone is too cowardly to say no when they needed to?

_____

_____

A controller expects you to be responsible for things that are their responsibility, such as keeping them happy. What happens when you try to fulfill their expectations?

Describe a situation in which you felt someone else was asking you to be responsible for what was their own responsibility. How did you respond?

Describe a situation in which you expected someone else to be responsible for what was your own responsibility. How did they respond?

How can a parent teach their child to take responsibility for their own life?

In a marriage, what happens if a controlling spouse is never confronted?

If you fulfill your number one responsibility in life, how will that impact all of your relationships?

According to John 13:8, what is required to have a healthy, fulfilling relationship?

Why does being a people-pleaser require that you be a phony?

To be authentic, what does Ephesians 4:15 state that you must do?

How do you please people in a healthy, balanced way?

_____

_____

Take Strength in God's Word

Read the Churchill quote at the beginning of this chapter. How does pleasing people rather than God cost us greatness?

_____

_____

Read 1 Kings 22:13–18, noting verse 13. What people-pleasing decision was the prophet Micaiah asked to make that would have cost him his greatness?

_____

_____

What basic principle did Jesus lay down in Matthew 5:10 that encourages you to not give in to pleasing people?

_____

_____

To become great, what must you do, and what must others do as well?

_____

_____

Authenticity in Action

If you have been a people-pleaser, you can decide today that no matter what it costs, you will do your best to follow your heart instead of a person. Making a change in that kind of relationship won't be easy, but you can do it.

With one person you have been trying too hard to please in mind, write out how you envision utilizing the three-step process.

1. Have a conversation.

_____

_____

2. Communicate clearly and responsibly.

_____

_____

3. Assess the response.

_____

_____

Write out a declaration that you are making a commitment to be your most authentic self as well as searching for friends who allow you that freedom.

_____

_____

Keep This in Mind

We must obey God rather than human beings!

Acts 5:29

To be your most authentic and unique self, make the decision that you will always do your best to follow your heart instead of people, no matter what it costs.

CHAPTER 16

Overcoming the Fear of Rejection

Get in Touch with Your Uniqueness

Whoever listens to you listens to me; whoever rejects you rejects me; but whoever rejects me rejects him who sent me.

Luke 10:16

What makes rejection such a powerful weapon to keep you from living as your authentic self?

_____

_____

What is the most significant way that the fear of rejection has stopped you from embracing your uniqueness and sharing it with others? When did it start?

_____

_____

Read Luke 9:1–5 and 10:1–11, and John 15:20 and 25. What instructions did Jesus give us about rejection and how to handle it?

_____

_____

According to John 6:37, what can you know for certain when you face rejection?

_____

_____

What does it mean to have a root of rejection, and what does it cause?

_____

_____

Take Strength in God's Word

Describe what Proverbs 29:25 says is the result of living in the fear of man.

_____

_____

Read 1 Samuel 13:1–14. What caused King Saul to disobey Samuel's instructions, and what was the tragic result?

_____

_____

Read about the second time Saul disobeyed God in 1 Samuel 15:1–26. What were the exact words Saul used to excuse his behavior? What did it result in?

_____

_____

Authenticity in Action

Take some time to think about how much you care about what people think of you. What is the truth about what they think?

_____

Would you say that your determination to succeed and achieve in life is driven from a desire to prove that you have worth and value? Explain your answer.

_____

What vital lesson can you take away from the story of David Brainerd? How can you keep your life in balance?

_____

According to Ephesians 3:17, what will make you immune to the agony of rejection?

_____

Write out Romans 8:31 and Psalm 118:6, then take some time and ask God to renew your thinking to believe His Word rather than feelings that arise.

_____

If the foundation of your life is rejection rather than acceptance, what are its repercussions when you are with other people?

_____

What is the only antidote to becoming a victim of rejection?

_____

To be authentic, we need to be healed from the fear of rejection and from insecurity, and God is an expert at healing these painful emotional conditions. I encourage you to open your heart and write a short prayer below to receive healing for whatever you need, inviting Him into every area of your life, especially the ones you have kept hidden.

_____

The next time you face rejection, what must you keep in mind in order to stand strong and walk in the freedom of being your unique self?

_____

Keep This in Mind

Those the Father has given me will come to me, and I will never reject them.

John 6:37 NLT

You will face rejection with its pain, but keep in mind that you already have the acceptance and love of the most important person in your life—Jesus.

CHAPTER 17

Authenticity Requires Integrity

Get in Touch with Your Uniqueness

The integrity of the upright guides them, but the unfaithful are destroyed by their duplicity.

Proverbs 11:3

Integrity is integral to living an authentic life. What does *integrity* mean?

_____

_____

On a scale of 1 to 10, with 1 being "poor and inconsistent" and 10 being "doing what's right even if no one is watching," how do you think you measure up to your definition of *integrity*? Explain.

_____

_____

In what ways have you built your life upon the principles of integrity, such as Proverbs 28:20?

_____

_____

What are we tempted to do when things seem to go well even after we've compromised our integrity in an area of our life?

_____

_____

Take Strength in God's Word

What do Proverbs 12:17 and 22 tell us about one aspect of integrity?

_____

_____

Name some ways that it is easy to cheat. Do you struggle with any of these?

_____

_____

What do the following verses teach you about honesty?
Psalm 15:4

_____

_____

Ephesians 4:25

_____

_____

Hebrews 6:18

_____

_____

Take some time to consider whether you are in the habit of saying whatever you need to say to avoid trouble. When do you struggle the most with this?

_____

_____

How does telling the truth force you to face the truth and be set free (John 8:32)?

_____

_____

Read Luke 9:23. In the context of keeping your word with integrity, what does it mean to follow Jesus?

_____

_____

Read 2 Timothy 4:8. What is the purpose of studying God's Word?

_____

_____

Read 2 Corinthians 5:20. What does it mean to be an ambassador for Christ?

_____

_____

Authenticity in Action

When we are trying to impress people, it's easy to say things and make promises that we really don't mean. Describe a situation where you did that and then had to be accountable for what you said.

_____

_____

What are the key words in Psalm 26:11 (NKJV)? Explain why.

_____

_____

What does the apostle Peter say you are called to be (1 Peter 2:9; 2 Peter 1:3)? What does that mean?

_____

_____

When you do something with excellence, does that mean perfectly or with extravagance? Describe what it looks like.

_____

_____

Based upon Isaiah 12:5 (NKJV), how should you be doing your life?

_____

_____

Read Daniel 5:12 (NKJV). Describe a person who has an "excellent spirit."

_____

_____

Do you have an "excellent spirit"? How can you improve in this area?

_____

_____

What does Philippians 1:9–11 (NKJV) teach you? Are you willing to make a commitment to excellence? I encourage you to write a declaration here.

_____

_____

Do everything you do with all of your heart, always giving your best, being your unique self, knowing that God is watching, and so is the world.

Keep This in Mind

As for me, I will walk in my integrity.

Psalm 26:11 NKJV

To be authentic and unique, always do what you say you will do, be honest in every way, tell the truth, walk in integrity, and be excellent, even if it hurts.

PART 3

Moving Forward as the Real You

CHAPTER 18

Pure in Heart

Get in Touch with Your Uniqueness

Blessed are the pure in heart, for they will see God.

Matthew 5:8

Why is it true that a person who is pure in heart is an authentic person?

_____

_____

What did Jesus mean when He said that the pure in heart will see God?

_____

_____

How does Matthew 5:8 (MSG) clarify the meaning of being "pure in heart"?

_____

_____

What relationship does a pure heart have to your faith?

_____

_____

Of the list of hindrances that can block your faith, which ones do you struggle with the most?

_____

_____

What is it that allows you to release your faith to be a true spiritual force?

_____

_____

Being authentic requires that you live in agreement with God's desires for you. What does that involve?

_____

_____

How would you apply that principle to what God's Word teaches you about forgiving others?

_____

_____

Take Strength in God's Word

According to John 8:31–32, what is the way to know yourself and find freedom?

_____

_____

What is the most difficult truth about yourself that you have faced? What has been the result of taking responsibility for your actions?

_____

_____

Write out the first half of Psalm 51:6 (AMPC) and begin to commit it to memory.

_____

_____

Read 1 Samuel 13:14 and Acts 13:22. After David committed such reprehensible acts, how could God still refer to him as a man after His "own heart"?

_____

_____

What do the following verses teach us about bringing hidden sin into the light?

James 5:16 (AMPC)

_____

_____

Proverbs 28:13

_____

_____

Psalm 85:15 (NKJV)

_____

_____

What do the following verses state you need to know about yourself through listening to yourself?

Matthew 12:34

_____

_____

Jeremiah 17:9

_____

_____

James 1:26

_____

_____

Obadiah 3

_____

_____

Romans 12:3

_____

_____

1 Peter 5:6

_____

_____

Authenticity in Action

You can help yourself grow by letting your words expose what is in your heart, then ask God to help you deal with it so you can become more like Him. For example, what do you say when a friend is blessed in a way that you are not?

_____

_____

What words do you use when you compare yourself with others? Are they words that are meant to help you feel good about yourself?

_____

_____

When you face difficult times, what does your conversation reveal about you?

_____

_____

Read Titus 1:15. What do the pure in heart believe about other people?

_____

_____

How does this truth help us deal with issues of trusting people?

_____

_____

Read 1 Corinthians 13:4–7. When someone is rude to you or hurts your feelings, how can the apostle Paul's teaching on love help you avoid being offended?

_____

_____

Based on 1 Timothy 1:5, how is an "unfeigned faith" an authentic faith?

_____

_____

Why we do what we do is more important to God than what we do. He wants us to have a pure heart, as in pure motives (reasons) for our actions. Take some time to consider your motives for what you do. For instance, write down why you go to church, give to a charitable cause, or spend time in prayer.

_____

_____

What sobering truth is taught in 1 Corinthians 3:13–15?

_____

_____

Read Matthew 6:1 and 2 John 1:8. How do "rewards" relate to your motives?

_____

_____

God's will is that you not lose any rewards and that you avoid doing things merely to please people when those actions do not reflect God's will for you. That unity within your life will lead to an authentic life with passion and zeal.

Keep This in Mind

You're blessed when you get your inside world—your mind and heart— put right. Then you can see God in the outside world.

Matthew 5:8 MSG

Keep your outer life consistent with your inner life, and you will find faith to carry you through every situation and into a place of victory with authenticity.

CHAPTER 19

Your Inner Life

Get in Touch with Your Uniqueness

I know of nothing more valuable, when it comes to the all-important virtue of authenticity, than simply being who you are.

Charles Swindoll

What is it that the apostle Peter makes so abundantly clear in 1 Peter 3:3–4?

_____

_____

What was your immediate response to this emphasis on your inner life? Would you say that it is true for you? In what ways is it, and in what ways is it not? How would you like to see improvement in this area?

_____

_____

If your emphasis is on your outer life, what does it do to your authenticity and living out your uniqueness? What did Jesus warn about this in Luke 12:2–3?

_____

_____

God sees the hidden person of the heart. How does He want you to be beautiful?

_____

_____

In what ways do you find yourself wearing different masks for different people and different situations?

_____

_____

Take Strength in God's Word

What stern words did Jesus speak to pretenders in Matthew 23:13–36?

_____

_____

When it comes to our natural life and our spiritual life, what must be our priority?

_____

_____

What do the following verses teach you about the inner and outer life?
2 Corinthians 4:16

_____

_____

Habakkuk 3:17–19

_____

_____

Revelation 3:17; 2:9

_____

_____

Define "the kingdom of God." Where does Luke 17:21 (NKJV) state that it is?

_____

_____

Take some time to prayerfully consider 1 Corinthians 3:16. What are your thoughts as you try to comprehend the profoundness of this?

_____

_____

What are some ways you can make the Holy Spirit comfortable in your life?

_____

_____

Authenticity in Action

First Peter 3:4 (AMPC) states that a heart that "is not anxious or wrought up" is precious in God's sight. How much of the time are you quiet and peaceful on the inside compared to being anxious or agitated? Be honest in your assessment. How can you improve in this area?

_____

_____

What is going on in your inner dimension all the time? What happens when inner turmoil prevails over inner purity?

_____

_____

Slowly read Luke 11:39–41 (AMPC) and reflect on what it is saying to you. Consider especially what it means to dedicate your inner life to God. Write your thoughts below.

_____

_____

What are some boundaries you can set to help prevent people and the pressures of daily life from taking away your inner peace? What are some things you need to say no to?

_____

_____

God so strongly desires a relationship with us that He willingly sacrificed His Son for our sins. To fellowship with us, He wants a portion of our time and desires. Consider the Lamb of God slain before the foundation of the world for you, and then I encourage you to write a prayer of dedication of your inner life to Him.

_____

_____

Keep This in Mind

For indeed, the kingdom of God is within you.

Luke 17:21 NKJV

Always be more concerned with who you are on the inside than with who you are on the outside. What's inside of you is the real you!

CHAPTER 20

Be Filled with the Holy Spirit

Get in Touch with Your Uniqueness

The fulness of the Spirit is not a question of our getting more of the Holy Spirit, but rather of the Holy Spirit getting more of us.

Oswald J. Smith

When you read "be filled with the Holy Spirit," what do you understand this to mean to you personally?

_____

_____

To be filled with the Holy Spirit, what must you be empty of?

_____

_____

How does the Holy Spirit get more of you when He is already in you?

_____

_____

How do Ephesians 3:19 and 5:18 (AMPC) define the role of the Holy Spirit in your life? How much of you does He desire to occupy?

_____

_____

Would you say that you are full of God or full of yourself? Explain your answer.

_____

_____

What is necessary for the spiritual maturity of those who desire authenticity and want to embrace their uniqueness?

_____

_____

Take Strength in God's Word

Read 2 Corinthians 3:18. Describe the process involved in spiritual maturity.

_____

_____

What work needs to be done in you, according to Philippians 2:12–13? What is your role in the work?

_____

_____

Have you surrendered to God? If not, are you willing to do so now? Describe what you are dealing with in your heart.

_____

_____

Why must your mind be renewed, and how does that happen (Romans 12:2)?

_____

_____

What three parts make up who we are? What happens to us at death?

_____

_____

As ambassadors for Christ, how does God make His appeal to the world through us (2 Corinthians 5:20)? Why is head knowledge not enough?

_____

_____

Authenticity in Action

What does it mean to have a wounded soul? What has happened to a person's emotions, mind, and will as a result of the hurts inside?

_____

_____

Would you say that your soul has been wounded? In what ways? Describe what you have experienced.

_____

_____

Why is inner healing so necessary? What is it that only God can give you?

_____

_____

Read Mark 8:34. To be Jesus' disciple, what must you do?

_____

_____

Is it possible to be selfish and happy at the same time? How does 2 Corinthians 5:15 tell you that you can live an unselfish life?

_____

_____

How does God bring healing to your soul and freedom from your fears?

_____

_____

Read 1 Thessalonians 5:23. What is the difference between your spirit and soul?

_____

_____

From the list of "self" problems, name the five that you know you need to deal with the most and describe why that is.

1._____

2._____

3._____

4._____

5._____

To live unselfishly as Jesus' disciple (Luke 9:23) is a task too big for any human to tackle alone. I encourage you to write a prayer below. Ask God to work in and through you until selfishness is replaced with the same kind of love that God shows through Christ. Ask Him to fill you to the full with the Holy Spirit.

_____

_____

Keep This in Mind

Ever be filled and stimulated with the [Holy] Spirit.

Ephesians 5:18 AMPC

Always be willing to give every area of your life to be filled by the Holy Spirit, realizing that it is not a onetime event, but a process that will unfold over time as you walk with God.

CHAPTER 21

Enter God's Rest and Be Yourself

Get in Touch with Your Uniqueness

Our rest lies in looking to the Lord, not to ourselves.

Watchman Nee

Why is it impossible to be authentic unless you learn how to rest in the Lord?

_____

_____

What makes trying to be someone else so frustrating?

_____

_____

Describe a time when you tried to be like someone else. What compromise did it require you to make to your own uniqueness?

_____

_____

Entering God's rest is about learning how to rest in your soul. To what degree would you say you are at rest internally and not working, working, working?

_____

_____

Take Strength in God's Word

Prayerfully and slowly read Matthew 11:28–29. When our soul is at rest, what life-transforming confidence does it bring?

_____

_____

_____

Jesus says to come to Him and receive His rest. He invites you to be joined to Him and learn from Him. Have you done that? Describe your experience and where you are at today.

_____

_____

_____

Write out the first half of Genesis 1:31. In that His pronouncement includes you, what is God saying about you?

_____

_____

_____

God says He made you very good. In what ways do you believe that in your heart, and in what ways do you struggle to believe it?

_____

_____

_____

Authenticity in Action

What does it mean that resting in God is not a rest _from_ work, but a rest _in_ work? How can you apply this principle to your daily walk and know "It is good"?

_____

_____

_____

Read 2 Samuel 17. What does David's father sending him to feed his brothers teach us about how God works out His plan for us in our everyday activities?

_____

_____

_____

When you take a stand for what is right as David did, what can you expect by way of opposition, even possibly from those who are closest to you?

_____

_____

_____

Why does it never work to try to go to battle in someone else's armor, especially if you've never worn armor?

_____

_____

_____

Have you ever tried using someone else's abilities, personality, or resources to accomplish what you need to do? What outcome did it lead to?

_____

_____

_____

What confidence did David take into battle that you must take into your battles? Write a bold declaration, as David made to Goliath, that you can use every day to live in victory and in your uniqueness.

_____

_____

_____

Keep This in Mind

Let us therefore be zealous and exert ourselves and strive diligently to enter that rest [of God, to know and experience it for ourselves].

Hebrews 4:11 AMPC

Always remember that you cannot use someone else's abilities, personality, or resources to accomplish what you need to do. Being at rest, being confident in Christ, and being yourself are essential for any kind of victory in your life.

CHAPTER 22

Be Real

Get in Touch with Your Uniqueness

Always be a first-rate version of yourself, instead of a second-rate version of somebody else.

Judy Garland

How does our biological life differ from the spiritual life available to us in Jesus Christ? How is Jesus the real life for which we are searching?

_____

_____

Read 1 John 3:9, 4:7, and 5:1, 4, and 18. What stands out to you about what it means to be "born of God"?

_____

_____

According to Acts 17:28, what makes Jesus more to us than someone we read about and admire?

_____

_____

What did Jesus warn about counterfeit Christians in Matthew 7:22–23?

_____

_____

What does it mean for you to be a real Christian?

_____

_____

Take Strength in God's Word

What do the following verses make clear about a real Christian?
Matthew 7:16, 20

_____

_____

1 John 3:9

_____

_____

1 John 3:10

_____

_____

Galatians 5:16–23

_____

_____

2 Peter 1:4

_____

_____

2 Corinthians 5:21

_____

_____

Romans 14:17

_____

_____

1 John 1:7

_____

_____

Matthew 28:20

_____

_____

What warning does Jesus give to believers in Revelation 3:2 and 15–16?

_____

_____

How did the apostle Paul say to keep from becoming lukewarm in Romans 12:11 and 2 Timothy 1:6? How do you do that in your life?

_____

_____

Authenticity in Action

What is the fruit of a counterfeit or immature Christian?

_____

_____

_____

What is the fruit of a real, spiritually mature Christian?

_____

_____

What should you always look for in the lives of those with whom you think you want to be involved, spend time, and be friends? Why is this so important?

_____

_____

_____

To be authentic, what must your love be like (Romans 12:9)?

_____

_____

_____

How does Matthew 22:37–40 put a priority on walking in love? How can you make your love for others practical?

_____

_____

_____

Read 1 Corinthians 13:4–8 and 13. Write out the fruit that love is to bear in our lives.

_____

_____

_____

On a scale of 1 to 10, with 1 being "dry and tasteless" and 10 being "juicy and sumptuous," how do you rate the fruit of love in your life? Where would you like to improve your love the most?

_____

_____

_____

What is the only way we can continue to love others?

_____

_____

_____

Loving others involves a cost. What did it cost God?

_____

_____

_____

What price must you be willing to pay to love others that they might experience God's love?

_____

_____

_____

A counterfeit Christian may speak words of love, but how does 1 John 3:18 define a real Christian's love? What if it goes against your feelings?

_____

_____

_____

Will you let God love someone through you? I encourage you to write a prayer and ask God to bring someone to your mind or attention whom He wants to love through you. Make a commitment to be willing to pay the cost it will involve.

_____

_____

_____

When you are gone from the Earth, how do you want people to remember you?

_____

_____

_____

Keep This in Mind

Those who say they live in God should live their lives as Jesus did.

1 John 2:6 NLT

Always let your life and your love be real, sincere, and without hypocrisy.

CHAPTER 23

Be Confident

Get in Touch with Your Uniqueness

This is the confidence we have in approaching God: that if we ask anything according to his will, he hears us.

1 John 5:14

Why is this chapter on confidence placed so late in this book?

_____

_____

Reread the opening quote. Take a few moments to consider and write down the impact of what it says.

_____

_____

What amazing invitation is offered to us in 1 John 5:15? How real is our faith?

_____

_____

To live confidently and without fear controlling you, what must you first have?

_____

_____

Write down the sentence from Warren Wiersbe that states how God wants you to build your life in order to be confident.

_____

_____

Take Strength in God's Word

Confidence is actually faith; it is a belief that you are capable of doing something. What two things must you remember according to John 15:5 and Philippians 3:3?

_____

_____

What do the following verses tell you about your confidence in God?
Hebrews 4:16

_____

_____

James 4:2

_____

_____

Ephesians 3:20

_____

_____

Mark 9:23

_____

_____

Isaiah 54:17

_____

_____

Based upon these scriptures, what is the only certain way to being confident?

_____

_____

According to 1 John 4:18, if you lack confidence, what will dominate you? What then happens to your individuality and uniqueness?

_____

_____

Besides fear, what other torments does confidence protect you from?

_____

_____

Authenticity in Action

If you lack confidence, how can you begin to work to change your beliefs?

_____

_____

Do you have to *feel* confident to *be* confident? Explain your answer.

_____

_____

Read Romans 12:4–5 and 1 Corinthians 12:12–27. Especially within the church, what should your confidence keep you from doing and being?

_____

_____

What profound truth and promise did God give Joshua in Joshua 1:5?

_____

_____

How can you apply that truth to every challenging situation you face today?

_____

_____

What lesson can you take from God's statement to Gideon in Judges 6:12?

_____

_____

How is that lesson even more intensely reinforced by God's promises to Moses in Exodus 3:12 and 4:12, when Moses kept emphasizing his natural inabilities?

_____

_____

Have you allowed your own natural inabilities or weaknesses to hold you back from being confident enough to do what you feel God wants you to do? In what ways?

_____

_____

What do you feel God is saying to you about your confidence through this chapter? Prayerfully consider it, and write out your thoughts.

_____

_____

As your confidence in Christ grows, you will have the confidence to step out and do great things. As you do, what must you also always remember to do?

_____

_____

Keep This in Mind

As I was with Moses, so I will be with you; I will never leave you nor forsake you.

Joshua 1:5

Be bold, be strong, be confident, and let God amaze the world through you!

CHAPTER 24

Be Comfortable with God

Get in Touch with Your Uniqueness

Mental prayer is nothing else...but being on terms of friendship with God, frequently conversing with Him in secret.

Teresa of Avila

What was your first response to the question *Is it possible, or even right, to have a comfortable friendship with God?* Describe how you regard this.

_____

_____

_____

Does a friendship with God lessen the great reverence you should have for Him?

_____

_____

_____

What two amazing truths about the Holy Spirit are taught in John 14:17 and 26?

_____

_____

_____

Would you say that your relationship with the Holy Spirit is as close as Jesus says? In what ways do you want it to be closer?

_____

_____

_____

Take Strength in God's Word

According to James 2:23, what must you do to be "God's friend"?

_____

_____

Read 2 Corinthians 5:21. What does being made righteous mean?

_____

_____

According to the friendship Jesus has brought us into (John 15:15), what does He make known to us?

_____

_____

How does God want you to draw near to Him (James 4:8)?

_____

_____

Do you come to God that way, or do live with an underlying fear that God is angry with you and you're guilty about something? Explain your answer.

_____

_____

Read and meditate on Psalm 103:11–12 and 2 Corinthians 5:17. How does confessing these truths verbally help you build a new image of yourself?

_____

_____

Read Romans 7:14–8:1. We all experience failures and guilt. What is your only source of deliverance, and what brings the sense of condemnation to an end?

_____

_____

Authenticity in Action

Why does the devil not want you to understand your righteousness in Christ?

_____

_____

Based upon Hebrews 4:15–16, what should mark your coming to God?

_____

_____

What insights into the wonder of prayer do James 5:16 and 1 John 5:14 give you?

_____

_____

What boost in confidence does Romans 8:26–27 give you for prayer?

_____

_____

Having been made righteous by faith, what do you need to understand about your behavior? What promise can you hold to in Philippians 1:6?

_____

_____

How does Galatians 5:22–23 reflect how behavioral change comes to you?

_____

_____

When it comes to spiritual progress, where must your focus remain?

_____

_____

What simple steps can you take to change a weakness or fault?

_____

_____

Write out the second half of John 10:10 (AMPC). How does a right standing with God by faith fit into this?

_____

_____

Write out the amazing privileges we are given through our justification through faith in Romans 5:1–3 (AMPC). Do you have to earn any of these privileges?

_____

_____

I encourage you to ask God to continue to bring you deeper into His friend-ship. Write a prayer and ask the Holy Spirit to make Himself known to you, to help you to hear His voice, and for you to be comfortable to talk with Him all the time.

_____

_____

Keep This in Mind

I have called you friends, for everything that I learned from my Father
I have made known to you.

John 15:15

Always be authentically and uniquely you in your friendship with God.

CHAPTER 25

Believe

Get in Touch with Your Uniqueness

Whoever believes in him is not condemned, but whoever does not believe stands condemned already because they have not believed in the name of God's one and only Son.

John 3:18

Working through this guide, you have studied many truths on being your authentic and unique self, but one thing remains, which only you can do: *believe*. In John 11:40, what does Jesus tell us will happen when we believe? What are some of the daily blessings that come through believing?

_____

_____

_____

How does believing God and His promises make life simple?

_____

_____

_____

From the list of questions about what you have studied in this book, write down the five questions that you know you need to revisit to make sure you allow the truth of God's perfect love for you to transform the way that you live day to day.

1._____
2._____
3._____
4._____
5._____

Take Strength in God's Word

Read Matthew 8:5–13 and 9:28–29. Why is what you believe so powerful?

_____

_____

What lesson can you take from the father in Mark 9:17–27 for times when you struggle to believe? What does he teach you about being authentic with God?

_____

_____

Describe a current situation that you are struggling with doubts about, and express your honest thoughts to the Lord.

_____

_____

When you are waiting for God to answer a prayer, what can you be assured of based on 1 Thessalonians 2:13?

_____

_____

How does Romans 1:17 instruct you on how to live?

_____

_____

Authenticity in Action

When you are faced with fear and worry, what decision must you make despite what you may be seeing and feeling?

_____

_____

What is it that gives you the confidence to believe and to have faith?

_____

How does Hebrews 11:1 (AMPC) describe faith? When you don't see the result of faith immediately, what can you be assured that you have?

_____

God has given us more than five thousand promises in His Word. How are they received?

_____

To be authentically and uniquely you requires believing. In what ways?

_____

Is it true that you can have anything you decide to believe you will have? Explain.

_____

Whether you are a morning person or not, what is a great way to start every day?

_____

What does it mean to dread, and how does that drain our zeal?

_____

Do you routinely dread something? Describe it and its impact on you.

_____

How can you defeat dread and the devil?

_____

Write out John 14:1 and begin to commit it to memory. How does it simply answer your problems?

_____

_____

As we close, I recommend that you write a prayer asking God to continue to show you the pathway to living authentically and uniquely, being transformed by the entire renewal of your mind to think as God thinks.

_____

_____

Keep This in Mind

Though you have not seen him, you love him; and even though you do not see him now, you believe in him and are filled with an inexpressible and glorious joy.

1 Peter 1:8

The pathway to having joy and enjoying your life, enjoying your unique self, and enjoying God is believing.

CONCLUSION

I hope that through this study and my book I have given you the biblical information to live life authentically, with freedom to express your uniqueness. I trust that you're starting to see that you have much to give to the world, and now is the time to begin doing it. This can be a new day, a new beginning for you, so start to:

- Live to please God, not people.
- Love people, but don't let them control you.
- Be courageous enough to say no to requests from people when you don't believe you are supposed to do what they ask of you.
- Live with confidence, be bold, and don't fear rejection.
- Be free to be your amazing self.

Your life is a journey, and no matter where you are on your unique journey, make decisions that enhance the remainder of it. Your story is unique, and it isn't finished yet. There are chapters of your personal story yet to come. Someday your story will say "The End," and when it does, you can be satisfied that you've lived the best life you could have lived. You need not have regrets, and you can leave a legacy that will continue to benefit others for years to come.

Do you have a real relationship with Jesus?

God loves you! He created you to be a special, unique, one-of-a-kind individual, and He has a specific purpose and plan for your life. And through a personal relationship with your Creator—God—you can discover a way of life that will truly satisfy your soul.

No matter who you are, what you've done, or where you are in your life right now, God's love and grace are greater than your sin—your mistakes. Jesus willingly gave His life so you can receive forgiveness from God and have new life in Him. He's just waiting for you to invite Him to be your Savior and Lord.

If you are ready to commit your life to Jesus and follow Him, all you have to do is ask Him to forgive your sins and give you a fresh start in the life you are meant to live. Begin by praying this prayer...

Lord Jesus, thank You for giving Your life for me and forgiving me of my sins so I can have a personal relationship with You. I am sincerely sorry for the mistakes I've made, and I know I need You to help me live right.

Your Word says in Romans 10:9, "If you declare with your mouth, 'Jesus is Lord,' and believe in your heart that God raised him from the dead, you will be saved" (NIV). I believe You are the Son of God and confess You as my Savior and Lord. Take me just as I am, and work in my heart, making me the person You want me to be. I want to live for You, Jesus, and I am so grateful that You are giving me a fresh start in my new life with You today.

I love You, Jesus!

It's so amazing to know that God loves us so much! He wants to have a deep, intimate relationship with us that grows every day as we spend time with Him in prayer and Bible study. And we want to encourage you in your new life in Christ.

Please visit joycemeyer.org/salvation to request Joyce's book *A New Way of Living*, which is our gift to you. We also have other free resources online to help you make progress in pursuing everything God has for you.

Congratulations on your fresh start in your life in Christ! We hope to hear from you soon.

ABOUT THE AUTHOR

Joyce Meyer is one of the world's leading practical Bible teachers. A *New York Times* bestselling author, Joyce's books have helped millions of people find hope and restoration through Jesus Christ. Joyce's programs, *Enjoying Everyday Life* and *Everyday Answers with Joyce Meyer*, air around the world on television, radio, and the Internet. Through Joyce Meyer Ministries, Joyce teaches internationally on a number of topics with a particular focus on how the Word of God applies to our everyday lives. Her candid communication style allows her to share openly and practically about her experiences so others can apply what she has learned to their lives.

Joyce has authored more than 130 books, which have been translated into more than one hundred languages, and over 65 million of her books have been distributed worldwide. Bestsellers include *Power Thoughts*; *The Confident Woman*; *Look Great, Feel Great*; *Starting Your Day Right*; *Ending Your Day Right*; *Approval Addiction*; *How to Hear from God*; *Beauty for Ashes*; and *Battlefield of the Mind*.

Joyce's passion to help hurting people is foundational to the vision of Hand of Hope, the missions arm of Joyce Meyer Ministries. Hand of Hope provides worldwide humanitarian outreaches such as feeding programs, medical care, orphanages, disaster response, human trafficking intervention and rehabilitation, and much more—always sharing the love and gospel of Christ.

JOYCE MEYER MINISTRIES
U.S. & FOREIGN OFFICE ADDRESSES

Joyce Meyer Ministries
P.O. Box 655
Fenton, MO 63026
USA
(636) 349-0303

Joyce Meyer Ministries—Canada
P.O. Box 7700
Vancouver, BC V6B 4E2
Canada
(800) 868-1002

Joyce Meyer Ministries—Australia
Locked Bag 77
Mansfield Delivery Centre
Queensland 4122
Australia
(07) 3349 1200

Joyce Meyer Ministries—England
P.O. Box 1549
Windsor SL4 1GT
United Kingdom
01753 831102

Joyce Meyer Ministries—South Africa
P.O. Box 5
Cape Town 8000
South Africa
(27) 21-701-1056

OTHER BOOKS BY JOYCE MEYER

100 Inspirational Quotes
100 Ways to Simplify Your Life
21 Ways to Finding Peace and Happiness
Any Minute
Approval Addiction
The Approval Fix
Authentically, Uniquely You*
The Battle Belongs to the Lord
Battlefield of the Mind*
Battlefield of the Mind Bible
Battlefield of the Mind for Kids
Battlefield of the Mind for Teens
Battlefield of the Mind Devotional
Battlefield of the Mind New Testament
Be Anxious for Nothing*
Being the Person God Made You to Be
Beauty for Ashes
Change Your Words, Change Your Life
Colossians: A Biblical Study
The Confident Mom
The Confident Woman
The Confident Woman Devotional
Do It Afraid*
Do Yourself a Favor…Forgive
Eat the Cookie…Buy the Shoes
Eight Ways to Keep the Devil under Your Feet
Ending Your Day Right
Enjoying Where You Are on the Way to Where You Are Going
Ephesians: A Biblical Study
The Everyday Life Bible
The Everyday Life Psalms and Proverbs
Filled with the Spirit
Galatians: A Biblical Study
Good Health, Good Life
Habits of a Godly Woman
Healing the Soul of a Woman*
Healing the Soul of a Woman Devotional
Hearing from God Each Morning
How to Age without Getting Old
How to Hear from God*
How to Succeed at Being Yourself

Teenagers Are People Too!
Trusting God Day by Day
The Word, the Name, the Blood
Woman to Woman
You Can Begin Again
*Your Battles Belong to the Lord**

JOYCE MEYER SPANISH TITLES

Auténtica y Única (Authentically, Uniquely You)
Belleza en Lugar de Cenizas (Beauty for Ashes)
Buena Salud, Buena Vida (Good Health, Good Life)
Cambia Tus Palabras, Cambia Tu Vida (Change Your Words, Change Your Life)
El Campo de Batalla de la Mente (Battlefield of the Mind)
Cómo Envejecer sin Avejentarse (How to Age without Getting Old)
Como Formar Buenos Habitos y Romper Malos Habitos
(Making Good Habits, Breaking Bad Habits)
La Conexión de la Mente (The Mind Connection)
Dios No Está Enojado Contigo (God Is Not Mad at You)
La Dosis de Aprobación (The Approval Fix)
Efesios: Comentario Bíblico (Ephesians: Biblical Commentary)
Empezando Tu Día Bien (Starting Your Day Right)
Hágalo con Miedo (Do It Afraid)
Hazte un Favor a Ti Mismo…Perdona (Do Yourself a Favor…Forgive)
Madre Segura de Sí Misma (The Confident Mom)
Momentos de Quietud con Dios (Quiet Times with God Devotional)
Pensamientos de Poder (Power Thoughts)
Sanidad para el Alma de una Mujer (Healing the Soul of a Woman)
Santiago: Comentario Bíblico (James: Biblical Commentary)
*Sobrecarga (Overload)**
Sus Batallas Son del Señor (Your Battles Belong to the Lord)
Termina Bien Tu Día (Ending Your Day Right)
Usted Puede Comenzar de Nuevo (You Can Begin Again)
Viva Valientemente (Living Courageously)
* Study Guide available for this title

BOOKS BY DAVE MEYER

Life Lines